COURAGE OVER CONFIDENCE

COURAGE OVER CONFIDENCE

Managing Mind Chatter and Winning the Mental Game

Mitchell Greene, PhD

NEW DEGREE PRESS

COURAGE OVER CONFIDENCE
Managing Mind Chatter and Winning the Mental Game

ISBN
979-8-88926-655-6   *Paperback*
979-8-88926-657-0   *Hardcover*
979-8-88926-656-3   *eBook*

CONTENTS

INTRODUCTION

In the late 1990s, New York Yankees second baseman Chuck Knoblauch made headlines because of an epic fall from grace. What was his problem? The former Gold Glove Award winner could no longer accurately throw the ball from second to first base. The sports writers from my hometown had a field day, printing snarky, jabbing comments at every opportunity. Knoblauch had some form of mental block, causing him at times to underhand or even walk the ball to first base. On some occasions, the television cameras caught Knoblauch awkwardly staring at the baseball before he threw it, leading one columnist to write, "When [Knoblauch] has time to think, he stinks" (Greenberg 1999).

Back then, I was finishing up my doctoral studies in clinical psychology. I was mesmerized by Knoblauch's demise. I could not fathom how someone as successful as Knoblauch—a four-time all-star—was now unable to hit the broad side of a barn. Tragically, Knoblauch's throwing problems never really went away. A few years later, after a brief stint in the outfield on a few different teams, Knoblauch retired.

Before I knew sport psychology even existed, I tried to understand everything I could about Knoblauch's issue. Instead of focusing on my graduate school courses, I was hunting down research on performance slumps, choking, and "the yips." My curiosity continued even as I started out in full-time clinical practice. By day, I was providing counseling to children, adults, and families; by night, I was reading what the sport psychology experts were saying about how someone as good as Knoblauch could perform so badly. It was becoming clear to me that even players of his stature could still find themselves at the mercy of a fickle and fleeting confidence.

Now, some thirty years later, not a month goes by without a story being published about a high-profile athlete who struggles *à la* Knoblauch. Stars such as the Olympians Simon Biles, Mikaela Shiffrin, and Michael Phelps, as well as professionals Naomi Osaka and Ben Simmons, are revealing what it's like to have to produce results when the entire world is watching.

Shiffrin, after admittedly underperforming at the 2020 Beijing Olympics, said she knew she was "obviously good," but for some reason couldn't get herself to believe it (Minutaglio 2022). Miami Dolphins quarterback Tua Tagovailoa acknowledged going through a similar phase of self-doubt. He described looking in the mirror after a series of less-than-stellar performances and asking himself, "Do I suck?" (Loughran 2022). These great athletes are proof that no one—no matter how well-trained—is immune from being overwhelmed by negative thoughts and feelings.

In my practice, I see competitors, from junior to professional, who are feeling more vulnerable and more worried about their ability to perform than ever before. Many feel they have no ability to see their results as anything but a reflection on a pattern that does not just apply to athletes playing at his level. Even younger, less accomplished athletes are seriously questioning their abilities at a time when they should just be enjoying themselves. Kids as young as twelve describe feeling like failures if they don't show promise in "their sport" the way they are supposed to. The parents of those twelve-year-olds also have a lot to consider, as *their* minds can fill up with mind chatter too. They have been indoctrinated into a youth sports culture that encourages parents not to miss any early windows of opportunity to enable their "good" athlete to become a "great" one.

When did youth sports culture become such a pressure cooker? Some believe the intensity went into high gear in the 1970s in response to the performance of Romanian gold medal gymnast Nadia Comaneci. She scored a perfect ten on the uneven bars in the 1976 Olympics and made the cover of *Time* magazine, with the caption "She's Perfect." Interestingly, that historical moment—the first "10" ever in an Olympic gymnastics event—was so unprecedented that the scoreboard was unable to display the number; instead, they had to list Comaneci's score as "1.0." According to sports medicine physician Dr. Heather Bergeson, Comaneci's dominance played a big part in America's adoption of the Eastern Europeans ethos of "start young, train hard" that forever changed the way we develop young athletes in this country (TEDx Talk, 2018).

Of course, Comaneci's perfect ten is just one factor in the trend toward less free play and more competition that characterizes the current youth sports landscape. Michigan State psychologist Daniel Gould believes emphasizing competitive success at early ages is "the single biggest problem we face in contemporary youth sports." Gould worries our systematic use of a "professional model" flies in the face of the mounting evidence that kids who start competing young and specialize in one sport—rather than multiple sports—experience high rates of burnout, injuries, and emotional stress (2019, 81–82). It goes without saying that conversations about helping athletes and parents manage their mind chatter are long overdue.

Gould's research, as well as that of many others in the field of sport psychology, has shown that stars who specialized early, like Comaneci, Tiger Woods, Lebron James, and Serena Williams, are exceptions to the rule, not the norm. In fact, several large-scale studies point to the fact that world-class adult athletes more often played several sports as kids. Only later in their development did they focus on just one. Regrettably, a growing percentage of children stop playing sports a lot sooner than they otherwise might because they start early, specialize in one sport, and train year-round. The main reasons are because they are stressed and aren't having fun. Some believe the numbers are close to 60 percent.

THE PRESSURE ON KIDS TO BE GREAT

In my practice, I observe the relationship between nonstop, high-stakes tryouts, showcases and tournaments, and major bouts of chatter-filled stress. My younger clients—both kids and their parents—fear the consequences of saying "no" to what they feel is nonnegotiable. This includes signing up for the next tryout opportunity, attending any coach-recommended clinic, enrolling in summer camp to do more training, traveling to yet another tournament, or scheduling extra unplanned workouts despite suspecting their bodies need adopted is one you will come to learn from the following chapters about how to manage your own chatter-full mind.

THE ROLE OF SOCIAL MEDIA

A chapter on the state of sports would be incomplete without at least a brief mention of social media and its impact on chatter. Of course, some competitors actually benefit from seeing someone else's highlight reel and comparing their statistics to others. Also, many acknowledge that they profit from the inspiration they receive from watching their opponents and athlete heroes lay it all out on the field. I can't think of a better example of this than the late, great basketball superstar Kobe Bryant. Athletes from all sports, and all levels, quote Kobe talking about "Mamba Mentality." This mentality preaches that greatness, which he certainly demonstrated, is earned through attributes such as hard work, resilience, mental flexibility, and a never-give-up attitude.

Yet for a percentage of these athletes, scrolling through their social media feeds or checking statistics online leads to more negative self-talk than they can handle. This was exactly the issue for several members of a top ten college track team for whom I provided workshop instruction. Only minutes after completing their races, they had a team ritual of huddling around someone's phone to compare their performances to the times of other runners in the conference. One athlete voiced serious concerns about the effects this comparison ceremony had on her psyche. Her courage to speak up led others to admit that they also spent too much energy being distracted by other people's races instead of focusing on their own goals. They admitted that the more they thought about their post-race huddles, the slower they ran.

Although the research on social media's impact on athlete performance is scant, I concur with those who have suggested its main effect is to negatively skew an athlete's perception of their own ability while amplifying the capabilities of their opponents. The tragedy is that all the hard work, time, and energy spent toward scoring more touchdowns, improving one's batting average, winning more games, and beating an opponent can quickly be wiped away if an athlete is overconcerned about and overwhelmed by what they read online.

CHAPTER 2

WHY POSITIVE THINKING DOESN'T WORK

If you've struggled with unhelpful mind chatter, chances are, at some point, a coach or parent has told you to be more "positive" or stop thinking "so negatively." Maybe they even suggested you should "just be more confident." Although they were undoubtedly trying to help, they were following the flawed conventional thinking that replacing negative self-talk with positive self-talk would get you out of your slump. You needed to believe in yourself more, they said, and to do that, you had to cut out the negativity and start generating more optimism.

But the problem was not—and is not—you. The problem is that it's difficult, if not impossible, to generate happy thoughts when you are being bombarded by negative ones. Many of you can probably relate to a time when you felt frustrated and angry about how you played, and to be supportive, your teammates tried to get you to "not worry about it," telling you it's "no big deal." In your mind, however, your performance was horrific, and nobody could convince you otherwise.

Or, maybe you frequently tell yourself you aren't nervous for a match when you really know you are, or that a tournament's outcome doesn't matter when you really believe it does. You can't trick yourself into feeling competitively fierce. Your mind knows *why* you are trying to think positive thoughts—to drown out the negative ones! This applies to mind chatter too. Trying to convince yourself you are unfazed about an upcoming competition, when you are actually feeling extremely tense about it, turns out to be a totally ineffective and wrongheaded approach.

The research data back this up. In a study on the effectiveness of positive thinking, Wood et al. concluded that "repeating positive self-statements may benefit certain people but backfire for the very people who 'need' them the most" (2009 860). This is particularly true for those who tend to be more naturally nervous and worried. For those who always seem to look on the bright side of life, they may have no trouble truly believing in and benefitting from the positive statements they tell themselves. In my practice, I witness the frustration and discouragement of competitive athletes who are full of mind chatter but have been told by coaches, parents, or sport psychologists their success hinges on their ability to be positive. I understand that coaches often don't know what else to say to help an athlete feel better.

To every frustrated, discouraged, or distracted athlete who slips back into negative thinking even after all of your efforts to get "on top of" your doubting mind, this book is for you. I know how tirelessly you work on your craft, training by yourself when you have to, and working out during vacation when the rest of your family is off having a good time. I know your physio is just one text message away when you feel a strain, and many of you are watching video replays of your workouts and matches to try and spot the keys that will unlock your best performance.

Unfortunately, I also know that mind chatter is, in its own way, just as persistent as you are. Chatter is relentless; it will show up, rain or shine, and it couldn't care less that you push yourself as hard as you do. The good news is there are answers to your frustrations, and those answers lie within you. In the chapters that follow, I will show you how you can use what you already have inside to reduce chatter's impact on your performances and help you shine when the competition lights are on.

BEYOND "POSITIVITY": CATHERINE'S STORY

Catherine, a college junior and committed Division I athlete, had started out the past two seasons crushing her opponents. But as the races became more competitive, she became increasingly nervous and panicky, sometimes unable to avoid finishing at the back of the pack despite her ability to run times in practice that would have put her near the front. To make matters worse, Catherine believed her poor track performances were her fault for not staying positive and optimistic about her racing potential. Now, in her junior year, she had reached a point where she had to decide: Was it still worthwhile to keep running if her mind kept forcing her to shut down?

Catherine and her coach had tried multiple approaches to quell the voice inside of her that made racing such a terrifying experience. She initially liked the habit of writing down and reciting several positive self-statements the night before races, including "I am fearless" and "I know I'm capable of doing this." Catherine believed this evening ritual, which at times included listing the things she was grateful for, definitely helped her feel better in the moment.

She looked forward to the ritual of lighting a candle, turning down the lights in her room, and taking out her journal and favorite pen. "Those lists take my mind off racing," she said, "and I like the way they empowers me." But on the track, these strategies were not making her feel empowered; instead, they had started to lose their luster and were backfiring. Catherine's performance wasn't improving, and she started to feel as though she was letting her coach down. Her coach had been trying so hard to help her adopt a more positive frame of mind.

He had her repeat certain mantras as she walked to the starting line, such as "Be bold" and "Be confident," but those incantations were not working. Around this same time, Catherine also consulted with a mental skills coach on regulating her breath using mindfulness techniques. These breathing techniques produced success off the track, particularly around the stress of final exams. However, as with the positive self-statements, Catherine found that these skills didn't translate to the track performance she had hoped to achieve. Catherine even learned how to incorporate visualization the night before races, but it took a lot of effort, and she struggled to sustain an image of herself running past people as opposed to one of being passed by them. She became frustrated and annoyed by her inability to see herself in a better light, even when she was just sitting in her bed with her eyes closed.

After she finished second to last in a mile race, having run much slower than her best time, Catherine reached her breaking point. She was nowhere to be found after the race. Eventually, her coach found her sitting by a fence on the side of the track. Head down, Catherine was pulling on the grass beneath her feet. Her coach slowly approached and sat next to her, initially saying nothing; he thought it was best just to let her know by his quiet presence that he was there for her. After a few minutes, Catherine said with frustration, "Obviously I was way more nervous than even I realized." Then she addressed him. "Coach," she said, "I've tried everything, but I still keep sucking."

At her coach's recommendation, Catherine and I started to meet. In our first session, just one week after her disappointing mile race, Catherine confessed she didn't really think she could be helped at this point. I was keenly aware that it would not be beneficial to her if we immediately jumped into a conversation about running, so I made sure to take the time to get to know Catherine better. I could tell by the way she sat up and smiled that she appreciated we had not just launched into "running talk."

She was happy to tell me about her friends, her favorite family vacation spots, and her beloved bulldog, Sandy, who lived back home with her parents. She teared up when she talked about Sandy. She said the tears were because she missed her and the comfort she could provide at a time like this, when she was feeling so stressed.

When the conversation turned to running, Catherine said her track goals were simple. She said, "I want to run in races just like I run in practice." As we discussed her circumstances, I was curious to know why she had stuck it out this long despite her problems with nerves and consistency. Without hesitating, Catherine described her love for the hard workout days, training side by side with her teammates. She smiled as she recalled the sometimes silly, sometimes serious conversations they would engage in on long, hour-plus runs. She mentioned the bus rides to meets with the boys' team and added that she cherished the "amazing" feeling she got when she ran a fast time.

I told Catherine I had one clarification; I couldn't make race day feel just like practice, as much as we might both wish I could. I explained that hard training runs and competitive races are, psychologically speaking, different in several key ways. And because of this, it was unrealistic to expect that she would feel the same way in both instances.

To help clarify this point, Catherine and I made a list of the thoughts she tended to have during practice and a comparable list for when she was preparing to race. We wrote both lists on a whiteboard in my office.

Practice Thoughts	Race Thoughts
I hope Coach doesn't make us do an extra mile like last week.	What if I don't finish ahead of Meg?
I'm going to run with Meg because we both like to complain while we run.	I'll be so embarrassed if Lauren passes me on the first lap.
Lauren will probably go out too hard like she always does.	What if I don't score points for my team—again?
I'm going to see if I can keep up with Meg.	I'm scared of the pain I know is coming.

She noticed that during practice, any negative thoughts or worries she had were short-lived and only mildly uncomfortable. In hard workouts, when the going got tough, her instinct would be to try to prove she was one of the fastest, and she would tell herself to "go for it." And more days than not, she would perform well. Catherine also made the keen observation that in practice, her teammates were also fighting through the pain of heavy breathing and heavy legs. Knowing that helped her get through her own discomfort.

When we looked together at her list of race-day thoughts, Catherine said seeing it in big bold writing on my whiteboard was eye opening. She knew training days and race days were different, but the side-by-side comparison helped crystallize just how divergent her thinking was on one day versus the other. She noted how much energy she was spending trying to tamp down her fatalistic thoughts and feelings about her chances of doing well, despite always showing up in peak physical shape. I explained to her that this pattern was totally normal, but we needed to develop a plan that helped her manage her race-day doubts.

Like a lot of athletes who perform poorly under pressure, Catherine was haunted by her "mind chatter." Certainly, all the telltale signs were there, such as her preoccupation with what-ifs:

- "What if I again run slower than my fastest time?"
- "What if I stink and I lose to her again?"
- "What if I still can't score points for my team?"

Mind chatter had done to Catherine what it does to all athletes. It slowed her down when all of her hard work had been aimed at speeding her up. It also robbed her of the joy she could be experiencing if those mental gremlins weren't busy short-circuiting her attempts at being successful.

As mentioned, Catherine had tried breath work and visualization to quiet those whispers of doubt. However, what she and her coach spent most of their time on was getting her to, as she put it, "just believe in myself." I told her the mind chatter approach we would be using *did not emphasize believing in oneself.* This caught Catherine by surprise. I wanted her to understand what I learned from both research and practice. It is a myth that athletes *must* have self-confidence if they are to have any hope of reaching their goals. Like most clients, Catherine had fallen prey to the notion that negative thoughts must be banished or turned into something more hopeful. This negative-to-positive replacement strategy, I explained, was making matters worse, not better.

I also shared with Catherine the tons of evidence that even elite athletes—those we admire for their mental toughness—still struggle with self-defeating thoughts. I described a conversation I had with an elite runner. He confessed that at the Olympic marathon trials, he seriously considered intentionally trying to trip over a curb to twist his ankle and avoid running because that way, no one could blame him for a bad result.

I could tell that relief and hope had entered the picture as Catherine began to see that having doubts didn't mean she was not prepared to race and fight to the finish. Before our conversation, Catherine didn't know there was any other way of dealing with her problem. "Instead of trying to get rid of doubts," I said, "we are going to welcome them in and ask them to join us for the ride." She laughed when I told her that

Rather, the chatter bell gets rung because it senses a different, more psychological form of danger; you might lose your sense of who you are or who you tell yourself you are supposed to be. You logically understand that you will physically survive whatever the outcome, but mind chatter still perceives the risk as one of life or death. Mind chatter's response is primal, not rational.

As one elite marathoner who felt his running had "plateaued" said, "I can never show my face back at work if I run slower than one of those up-and-coming nobodies." He happened to work at a running store, making the possibility of "losing" to one of his young, fresh-out-of-college workmates even more threatening. His chatter sensed his identity as "the fastest elite runner in the area" was on the line, making even "easy" runs more difficult. The threat to who he thought he was and needed to be caused him, in races, to breathe fast when he needed to breathe slowly, and to dial down his pace when he really needed to pick it up. He was able to grow as a person and a runner only when he came to appreciate that mind chatter was actually *taking away* his competitive drive by consuming him with overblown thoughts about how he might psychologically "die."

Mind Chatter Shows Up When the Stakes Are High

One reason your mind chatter might confuse you is because it isn't nearly as evident in practice as when you are in full-blown competition mode. And let's face it, you spend way more time training, working out, scrimmaging, doing drills, getting one-on-one lessons, and recovering than you do playing high-stakes games and tournaments. In these situations, mind chatter is mostly dormant because people do not care nearly as much about their practice results or mistakes that are not going to be publicized.

Mind chatter shows up under two conditions: when there is a good deal of uncertainty about the outcome and when the stakes are high. In other words, it is not a random phenomenon. A very common scenario in my practice is an athlete telling me they played the best they have played in a long time when facing an opponent who was undeniably, head-and-shoulders *better* than they were. They may report being chattery to start the match but mostly chatter-free once it got going. Why? The stakes of the match are low because a loss is of less consequence if the world is not expecting a win. Thus, you can play with minimal chatter since the "What will people think of me?" button has not been activated.

Conversely, playing against someone who, by all accounts, isn't as talented or skilled as you, but who you know is capable of winning, can lead to an increase in chatter. Why? It is because of the uncertainty about the outcome along with the fact that losing means a lot more than just another tally in the loss column. A loss means failure to meet expectations and potential public embarrassment. *You* might think it's worth the risk, but mind chatter, in its mission to shield you from pain and suffering, disagrees.

Mind Chatter Always Goes Overboard

Beyond the risk of merely not playing well, your mind chatter can get you to buy into the notion that what's on the line may be a circumstance from which you cannot recover. Many chattery their intentions rather than their internal dialogue, successfully socialize with others. The key was to accept that they weren't lacking in skills but rather had a very active and over imaginative "mind" that had them believing that people with whom they might interact would undoubtedly see them as weird or awkward. Many felt great relief from this group therapy, with one participant saying, "It's great to find out what actually helps. Despite my fear, I took a chance and decided to participate in life." Another said, "The second part of my life really began when I finally accepted that I was shy and withdrawn, and it was a waste of time to pretend otherwise."

The acceptance-based approach I teach athletes started from these classroom and interactive experiences in graduate school. In the same way we helped these shy adults, my methodology involves learning how to peacefully coexist with those bothersome elements of our internal dialogue.

- You've beaten your opponent twice before and are playing her again, but last time she almost won.

Even if you haven't experienced these particular high-stakes situations, you likely have your own examples of times when your competition-day jitters were triggered. Maybe you are a pro tennis or squash player and want to break into the top fifty in the world, or you are a minor league baseball player who may have a chance to get called up to the big leagues if you can stay consistent at the plate. Think about what circumstances, in your own experience, have led to a major case of game-day gremlins.

Going forward, I want preparing for chatter to be something you never leave off your pregame to-do list. If you are a softball player, you wouldn't show up to your game without a bat or glove. If you are a runner, you wouldn't forget your sneakers before a race. If you are a football player, you wouldn't go into a game without your helmet. It doesn't matter what sport you play. If it's go-time, it's also prepare-for-chatter-time.

RECOGNIZING THE SCRIPT

To prepare, I find it helpful to teach athletes to think of their mind chatter as scripted, much like the way a football coach might script his first ten plays of the game. With the help of a solid game plan, everyone on the team knows that no matter how many yards you gain, the next play is set in stone. If you have planned well for mind chatter's arrival, before or during a high-stakes game, you know you will be telling yourself a set of "lines" that reflect what you want to make happen, and your chatter will then feed you its own lines about what can go wrong. With proper planning, you start to realize the "inner game" isn't as elusive as you thought, and mind chatter's dramatic messages are just as predictable as that football team's first ten plays.

Let's say you are a skier who is a week out from your next big national race. What are the first lines of your "script"? Pre-race, you might remind yourself you have had, say, three solid weeks of practice, or you have done extra weight room work and are therefore much stronger than you were in your previous race. Maybe you would reassure yourself with a line or two about how "this is just one of many races" and you can "stop making a big deal of it." As an athlete, it makes sense to review and focus on your strengths, try and get perspective, and remember you have put in the necessary work. You may think this is enough self-encouragement to be ready to go, but it often turns out that it's not enough to have you *truly* ready to compete.

That is because, as the "scene" continues, your mind chatter inevitably kicks in, trying to put a damper on your confidence-building self-statements. It starts reciting its own lines, such as: "Oh yeah? I remember you said something similar the last time you needed to do well, and how did that work out?" or "What if you really are at your best and it isn't good enough?" No matter how encouraging, inspiring, and accurate your self-statements are, mind chatter will come in just as powerfully to argue the opposites. Although chatter can be frightening, painful, and difficult to hear, it is nothing if not predictable, so you do not need to let it take you by surprise.

I want to again emphasize that mind chatter's "job" is to protect you when it thinks you are under threat—whether from a poisonous berry or a potentially ego-crushing loss. Therefore, the lines it delivers should be heard from the perspective that they are primal, predictable, and ordinary, following a simple pattern you can learn to spot. Knowing your chatter will be doing its best to refute every encouraging notion you have about yourself can allow you to take it less seriously. Once you see where the mind chatter script is going, it is harder for any given line to cause harm.

PUTTING IT INTO PRACTICE

Marcy, a college swimmer, was growing frustrated with her uneven race results. She had proven to be a very good swimmer, even qualifying for the Olympic trials, but admitted she did not feel like a very good *competitor*. The moment her mind chatter rolled in, Marcy explained, she would "roll over."

Marcy said that when she heard the term *mind chatter* used as a way to describe that "other" voice in her head, she started to feel more optimistic. As someone who already journaled as a means of self-expression, she appreciated the value of putting pen to paper. Marcy took well to her first written assignment, an exercise that highlighted the predictability of mind chatter. About a week before a big race, I asked her to write down what she expected her chatter to say on the morning of the competition. After the race, she was to write, to her fullest recollection, a list of what her chatter actually did say. We would then be able to look at these lists side by side in our next session.

You can see the two lists below. A check mark (✓) indicates a correct prediction, and a circle (O) means her chatter had stayed quiet on that point. Note that on race day, mind chatter came up with a few more thoughts than Marcy had anticipated. Those are marked by an exclamation point.

Marcy's Mind Chatter Predictions [Monday]		Marcy's Race Day Mind Chatter [Saturday]
What if my legs feel heavy?	✓	What if my legs feel heavy?
What if I feel like I can't catch my breath?	○	What if I feel like I can't catch my breath?
I can't afford not to PR in this race.	✓	I can't afford not to PR in this race.
You cannot screw up your underwaters again.	○	You cannot screw up your underwaters again.
I think it's probably going to be the same bad result as last time.	✓	I think it's probably going to be the same bad result as last time.
	!	My coach has to see that I'm not going to fall apart.
	!	I don't want to let my team down again.

In the past, Marcy would try to wish mind chatter away and would therefore be caught by surprise when it showed up at her races. However, when she learned to get acquainted with what her chatter had to say in advance of big events, she began to see a payoff in her performances. Marcy had figured out what to expect. In lower-stakes competitions, she had fewer chattery statements to jot down, but in high-pressure battles, she had many more to list. The less energy she spent being shocked and overwhelmed by her chatter's arrival, the more competitive she became in the pool.

Doing this exercise yourself can help you become familiar with the scripted nature of your own mind chatter. You can use the blank chart below, or you can scan the QR code to access a version you can fill out on your device. My goal is to have you notice that those negative thoughts are actually part of a familiar and unavoidable script. Here's how to do it:

1. At least several days before your competition, write down what you think your chatter might say later in the week when the stress of competition feels like it's "on top of you."

2. When you are a day or so away from game day, write down again what your chatter is saying and see how it matches up to what you wrote down earlier in the week. Is your chatter offering any surprises, or is it giving you a hard time about the things you thought it would?

Mind Chatter Predictions [_____day]	Competition Day Mind Chatter [_____day]

The goal of this exercise is to help you cut down on those "OMG I can't believe I'm so nervous" moments as the competition draws closer. There are a lot of things you can't control when you are a competitive athlete, such as how well your opponent will play and even whether you will win or not. However, this type of chatter planning is something that *is* under your direct control.

The exercise I am recommending may help you come to realize what Marcy became more aware of during this process, which is the difference in thinking between "good" and "bad" races. Marcy noticed that in races where she competed at the level she knew she was capable of, her pre-race chatter had thrown up relatively few red flags for her to worry about. Her poor performances, though, had been preceded by a laundry list of chattery predictions. Pre-race planning for you should take on a new flavor as you start to recognize when your mind chatter is bound to be especially active. The biggest payoff will be that you won't be caught off guard when chatter shows up right before a big event, giving you every reason in the book why you should expect the worst.

ISN'T IT BAD TO "THINK NEGATIVE"?

Some people have questioned the rationale of spending any time at all focusing on their mind chatter. Why would they start reflecting on their negative thoughts so early in the week before a big competition? A common refrain from athletes is: "I try *not* to think about the game because it's only going to make me more nervous." In contrast with the approach I suggest, they convince themselves that thinking about "bad stuff" is only going to get it to multiply.

I understand those concerns. My job is to help you manage your mind chatter, not instigate more of it. However, there are two points to consider. First, it is likely that mind chatter is already present, even if you aren't actively engaging with it. Second, there's a difference between creating chatter and increasing your awareness of it. So, how might you know if it's already there? Here are a few clues:

- You have trouble sleeping the week or two before a game because you can't "get out of your head."

- You have significant inconsistencies in recent performances and your coach tells you it's not due to your technique or physical abilities.

- You are performing significantly better in practice than in games.

- You feel sick to your stomach and perhaps throw up before events.

- You sometimes wish, pre-tournament, that you were injured or had an excuse to stay on the bench.

Grant, a fun-loving triathlete who liked to keep his negative thoughts locked away in the closet, came to me when, after going professional, his mind chatter had become impossible to ignore. I knew that in order to help Grant, I would have to teach him how to open that closet door, face his mind chatter monsters, and regain control of his game-day mindset.

A coach had advised grant to ignore what he was feeling, dismiss his negative thoughts, and view race day as "just another long, hard training day." Grant tried to follow that advice and pretend he felt fine, just as he had when competing as an amateur athlete. But now that he was a pro, he knew his competitors in any race would be just as talented and prepared as he was. No matter what he told himself, Grant's chatter was not so easily put off.

For the first time, Grant started to plan for his mind chatter. In itemizing the stakes in these professional races, he first listed some obvious ones. These included the need to bring home a "paycheck," please his sponsors, and rank among the fastest swimmers. But as we dug deeper, he recognized the full extent of the pressure he was putting on himself. He feared disappointing his wife and his coach—as well as himself—and worried he was wasting his life on what people might see as a selfish pursuit.

Grant realized he could not just pretend to not have these concerns, nor could he cover them up with positive thinking. He needed a system with steps to follow to manage his mind chatter. Grant came to see his chatter's arrival not as a sign of weakness but simply as a function of the fact that his races had taken on a new importance in his life. His job was not to ignore his chatter but to make sure it didn't rule and ruin the day. Together, we made a mind chatter management plan that would help him prepare for that job.

AVOIDING THE "DOUBLE WHAMMY"

Here's my final argument for why planning for mind chatter is so important. When you aren't prepared, you leave yourself wide open to the strong possibility that you will have a double dose of chatter. In other words, *you will have mind chatter about the fact that you have mind chatter*—a double whammy.

Here's an illustration of how a double-whammy conversation sometimes unfolds between an athlete and their chatter.

Athlete: I'm ready. I feel like today is going to be my day.

Mind Chatter: You said that last weekend at the other tournament.

Athlete: I did, but hey... new day, fresh start.

Mind Chatter: What if you start out playing badly again?

Athlete: Geez, I can't believe I'm thinking so negatively again. I was trying to be positive and now look at what I'm doing! Why do I suck so much that I can't even give myself a pep talk?

Mind Chatter: This isn't going to go well.

Athlete: This isn't going to go well.

Notice how quickly the athlete starts to have chatter about their chatter? Denying chatter only elicits more of it. It also leads you to believe the chatter is the problem, instead of remembering that chatter is normal—a predictable symptom of uncertain, high-stakes competitions. When you reject chattery thinking, you not only skip over the first step in mind chatter management—anticipating and accepting that negative thoughts are coming—but also run the risk of having negative thoughts about your negative thoughts—a "double whammy."

FINAL THOUGHTS

The take-home message is that the monsters in the closet aren't so scary once you open the closet door. If you have ever spent your energy avoiding mind chatter or fighting with yourself because you have it, it's time to get ahead of your chatter by seeing it for what it is—a protective mechanism that cares about your psychological and physical survival. It exaggerates the consequences of a potentially poor performance because it doesn't want to see you lose what you have gained or have others think badly of you. It shows up in high-stakes situations as predictably as the lines in a familiar film script. Realizing mind chatter is not worth fighting with, and it's only playing its part, is the first step toward knowing how to manage it rather than feeling like it is managing you.

PLANNING FOR CHATTER'S ARRIVAL: TAKE-HOME TIPS

- Athletes who try to convince themselves to treat a high-stakes competition as just another event on their calendar are fooling themselves but not their chatter. Your chatter will win almost every time you try to treat a competition as unimportant when you know it's potentially a big deal.

- Some think that planning to "play angry" can bring out the best in them. Though feelings of genuine rage may have the effect of getting you "out of your head," I rarely have had an athlete tell me that this sort of "strategy" worked more than once. One athlete joked that she wished she could be dumped by a new boyfriend every week because in her last match, her anger about a breakup had helped her play her best. It's a funny idea, but not one you can count on. In other words, there are no "tricks" to becoming a consistent competitor.

- Chatter planning isn't just for before the competition starts. Even if your chatter has quieted down before a game, it will come roaring back when you drop a pass, double fault on breakpoint, strike out, or cause a turnover. Planning for chatter's arrival means planning for it to come both before and during the game, and sometimes even afterward.

- Some clients who successfully prepare mentally for one tournament figure that because it went well, they may not need to prepare as much for the next contest. However, the majority of athletes I serve are playing at a level where most games or tournaments present new challenges that require them to be at their best physically and mentally. Learning how to prepare is part of the discipline. It's also the case that the better you become as a competitor, the more likely it is that those you will face will be more skilled and talented, thus warranting better preparation on your part.

- Just because something seems like a significant athletic challenge to you, such as an Olympic trial, doesn't necessarily mean it will be high stakes for everyone. Some athletes are just "happy to have made it" and can compete in such an event without chatter holding them back. But the vast majority will regularly find themselves in situations that stir up their chatter.

CHAPTER 5

CHANGING YOUR RELATIONSHIP WITH CHATTER

1. *Expect and plan for mind chatter's arrival on the scene.*

2. *"Make room" for your chatter instead of resisting its message.*

3. *Identify and focus on specific, controllable "action goals."*

4. *Seek to perform with courage even when confidence is lacking.*

Now that you know when to anticipate mind chatter and how to prepare for its arrival, I'm asking you to take another brave step: Try to befriend your chatter. Remember from the previous chapter that mind chatter is not your adversary. While it may go overboard, it has a "legitimate" reason to exist. Mind chatter is trying to protect you, even though it might make you feel uncomfortable or insecure. You can think of your chatter as a wayward friend, difficult coworker, or troublesome family member; although you may not see eye to eye, you can still find a way to get along.

The fight you have been having with your chatter may be the very reason you haven't yet become the competitor you are capable of being. Perhaps you have been doing the opposite of what I'm proposing, trying *not to think* about your chatter's gloomy predictions and probably failing. Maybe you are saying to yourself, "I'm just going to pretend it's not even there." Or you might just be *hoping* your chatter will lessen or disappear when you get to the field, telling yourself, "I'll be fine; I'll wait and see if it goes away on its own." Some of you have probably tried to *drown out* your uncomfortable thoughts with positive affirmations, such as "I am tough," "I can and will dominate," and "I will not be afraid." Each one of these strategies is a way of fighting with your chatter; but no matter which you choose, you are entering a fight that you *will not* win.

The approach I am proposing might very well be a 180-degree turn from how you previously attempted to handle self-defeating thoughts and feelings. It may take time to fully grasp, but with practice, you will learn that the energy you have spent battling chatter can instead be channeled toward helping you get a hit when the bases are loaded, bring your relay team into the lead, or make a key save to preserve the victory.

WELCOMING IN ALL OF YOUR THOUGHTS

The reason fighting chatter by using those avoidance strategies doesn't work is because trying *not* to think of something— resisting it—only gets you thinking more about it. Take a few moments and try *not* to think about your tongue. Ready? Go. How did you do? Despite my instructions, I'm guessing it didn't take long for your attention to shift to your tongue. Maybe you began thinking about how large it is for such a small space

means "everything is right on schedule." Although chatter may have you thinking and feeling like you are in some kind of jeopardy, you can remind yourself that this is to be expected. As the stakes get higher, chatter gets louder.

Chatter has a knack for showing up at the worst times, but its appearance should signal to you that things are moving along their expected course. Using your previous approach, you may have viewed your big-game chatter as a sign that you were in big-game trouble. This is not the case. Next-level competitors reverse that way of thinking, *expecting* significant amounts of chatter and reminding themselves that things are playing out just as predicted.

I gave this advice to a rower who was experiencing mind chatter as she prepared for her two-kilometer time trial. When chattery voices bubbled up, I explained, she should consider them as much a normal "part of the test" as strapping in her feet, getting comfortable on the seat, and resetting the timer to zero. This simple suggestion was so different from how she typically handled stressful time trials that she couldn't believe what I was asking her to do. She told me her mind was "blown" by this new way of thinking.

I asked her to be willing to put "Make room for chatter" at the top of her pre-time trial checklist, and then I told her one more thing. At the first sign of chattery trouble, she should look at her watch and say to her chatter, "I see you are right on time." I also suggested she try saying the "you are right on time" line while doing her best British accent. Sound ridiculous? I wanted to reinforce the idea that she could "play" with her chatter even though its message was so serious and ominous. What's more, it made her laugh.

You might be wondering if she was still nervous when taking the timed test. The answer is yes, of course she was. The difference was that she had learned she didn't need to waste extra energy trying to pretend like she was calm. Ironically, when you accept that you are nervous, those jittery feelings may automatically begin to decrease. On the other hand, if you attempt to get rid of them, they will definitely be amplified.

Welcoming Chatter as a Guest

So far, we have made room for our mind chatter and acknowledged, with its utterly recognizable messages, it shows up at exactly the "right worst time." My clients have further benefited from viewing chatter as a house guest who shows up even though they didn't want visitors. In the past, your instinct may have been not to answer your door when chatter came knocking. But chatter is a persistent bugger who will just keep banging on the door. Sooner or later, you'll have to let this guest in. Why not open the door and be done with it?

Imagine you are getting ready for your semi-final match, and you hear mind chatter's familiar "knock" on your mental "door." You invite your "guest" in, suggesting they hang around if they want. This sort of guest isn't going to encourage you, cheer for you, or provide you with cues on where to focus during the game. In fact, your guest will likely be quite impolite.

- If you are a baseball player, your "guest" will complain that one more poor at-bat will have you benched.

- If you are returning from injury and cleared to resume full contact, your "guest" will remind you that you could reinjure yourself.

- If you are trying out for a team, your "guest" will get you to think about how embarrassed you'd be if you were the *one person* who didn't make it.

Guests like these cannot be ignored, but they are much less annoying if you don't take their comments to heart.

Those who practice mindfulness would say this fits the concept, derived from Asian religious philosophies, that whatever is resisted will persist. And, whatever you just let be, will, in turn, let you be. Opening the door to your chattery guest means you are accepting that chatter will take up some space where you live. That's better than hearing someone continually banging on your door!

This way of managing chatter worked very well for a hockey player who, after years of hard work, finally got called up to the pros. His chatter had always been an unhelpful sidekick, even though he was a star player. He had it in his head that this time, in front of "real" crowds and getting paid "real" money, he was doomed because his worries and second-guessing would be at an all-time high. He wondered how quickly people might realize he was not really "pro material" and should be shipped back down to the minors.

Unlike Grant, the professional triathlete I described in chapter 4, whose denial of his own mind chatter left him unprepared for its arrival, this hockey player saw his chatter coming from a mile away, but he had no clue what to do when it showed up. His default response was terror, treating chatter as a threat he needed to hide from if he was to stay safe. I was able to show him that because chatter was bound to eventually find him, he needed to get out ahead of it and face it head-on. He liked the idea of making room for chatter by "shaking hands" with it. This was a totally new way to think about his relationship with his doubts and worries. Like repeating a mantra to himself, he would "shake hands" with his chatter, as many times as he needed to, each time it found its way to the front of his mind.

BUT AM I LETTING CHATTER WIN?

It should be clear that I want you to move away from thinking of chatter as an inconvenience and negative feelings as signs that you can't perform well. Unfortunately, most of the strategies I see athletes using or sport psychologists advocating imply that the doubt you are experiencing is *not the way you are supposed to feel*, as if you are going about the whole "mental game" thing the wrong way. But just as you shouldn't feel confident being on a boat during an ocean storm, you shouldn't be expected to feel resolute and unflinching when the conditions for mind chatter—uncertainty and high stakes—are in place. In other words, you might be charging yourself with psychological crimes that you have not committed. Although chatter goes completely overboard, it is a protective instinct, plain and simple. It's as natural as your body sweating in the heat to cool itself off or shivering to keep itself warm when you are cold.

I often hear athletes say, "But I should be more mentally tough by now." Being mentally tough does not mean you will be chatterless; rather, it's the ability to keep chatter from derailing you the "park it" strategy has the benefit of generating a visual image that gets right to the point and can be conjured up with just a few words.

PUTTING IT INTO PRACTICE

Just like golfers need to practice putting to get better at controlling their swing and reading the greens, making room for your mind chatter also takes practice. You are literally "flipping the script," getting rid of your old way of talking to chatter and developing a new way of dialoguing with it.

In your old way of doing things, you might have responded to a chattery "what if" question with a response that showed you didn't think it was okay for chatter to question you that way. Maybe your conversation-with-self said, "This is bad. I'll just start thinking more positively." Or you slipped into a double-whammy situation where you heard your chatter and thought the fact that you were having chatter was a bad sign, which led you to have chatter about that too.

Your new approach, which you can rehearse below, has you changing your relationship to your chatter so that you answer "What if?" questions with a response that shows you knew chatter would eventually arrive. In the exercise below, I want you to use your renovated set of management tools and flip the script on your old dialogue with chatter.

Exercise 1: Flip the Script

Previously, you might have responded to chatter with thoughts that showed a lack of preparedness for its typical "This isn't going to end well" predictions. Perhaps you can relate to the following example:

Athlete: I think I can beat her. I almost beat her last time.

Chatter: You always think you can beat someone you almost beat. But you usually lose.

Athlete: Ugh, it's true. Every time I tell myself I can beat someone, I end up losing.

Below is a sample script where the athlete has learned to "flip the script" and come back with a *helpful* response:

Athlete: I think I can beat her. I almost beat her last time.

Chatter: You always think you can beat someone you almost beat. But you usually lose.

Athlete: Ah, I see you, chatter. I figured you would have something negative to say. I appreciate the input, but I have more important things to take care of right now. I've got to get ready to play.

Now it is your turn. Use the following blank chart, or scan the QR code to complete the exercise on your device. Here are the instructions:

1. I want you to fill in a brief dialogue between you and your chatter. First, provide your typical response, the kind that doesn't show what you've learned about how to make peace with your chatter.

If you are willing to be chattery, emotional intensity tends to subside although this is not guaranteed.

- Some think that because they have reached the professional ranks, they should have outgrown the whole "nerves" thing. If anything, those who compete on the biggest stages often have the most to lose and therefore are the most susceptible to game-time anguish. The need to accept your mind chatter's existence applies to everyone, whether you are a "junior" player looking to make your first varsity team or a seasoned athlete who has already achieved considerable success. To be sure, no amount of experience, achievement, or hard work will totally prevent mental gremlins from invading your psyche.

- Here's one for the coaches, teammates, and sports parents. Telling a player "not to be nervous" may actually set them up for unnecessary inner turmoil. It suggests something is wrong with being nervous. It would be better to reinforce the message that nervousness is, for many, part of the game. Instead of shutting the conversation down by saying "don't worry about it," you can ask questions that give the athlete opportunities to share what specifically is concerning them. Creating space for these types of conversations is often a big part of getting the best out of your athlete.

CHAPTER 6

SETTING GOALS TO IMPROVE PERFORMANCE

1. *Expect and plan for mind chatter's arrival on the scene.*

2. *"Make room" for your chatter instead of resisting its message.*

3. ***Identify and focus on specific, controllable "action goals."***

4. *Seek to perform with courage even when confidence is lacking.*

With mind chatter under control, the question now is where to shift your attention so you can be locked in and game ready. Although you've made room for—and peace with—your chatter, you know how unwise it is to simply focus on those thoughts about losing, letting the team down, or making a fool of yourself. That would be the opposite of what I have been preaching. As performance expert Tim Gallwey recognized, in order to "still one's mind," you have to have somewhere to "put it" (1974, 75). That somewhere is on your goals.

The topic of goal setting can be confusing. There are multiple types of goals, such as outcome goals, performance goals, learning goals, motivational goals, and process goals. Athletes, coaches, and sport psychologists have strong opinions, both pro and con, about the value, utility, and potency of each. I have found it best to classify them into two broad categories—*results-oriented goals* and *action goals*. I will discuss each in turn and show you how to use them to your advantage.

RESULTS-ORIENTED GOALS

Results-oriented goals are those that concern either in-game achievements, such as getting on base two out of four times at bat or finishing an 800-meter track race in a specific time; or "big picture" results, such as winning the game, winning the tournament, or having your team advance to the next round of the playoffs.

Some in the sports world make a distinction between "outcome" and "performance" goals, but for our purposes, I have combined those two types of objectives into a single "results-oriented" category. The reason is because chatter, as a rule, attaches itself to both outcome- and performance-focused results, whether personal or team oriented, short or long term.

Results-oriented goals are not to be dismissed; they are essential to your growth and development as an athlete. But because mind chatter feeds on those wished-for outcomes, results-oriented goals must be handled with caution. You can't forget that mind chatter's fear-based pronouncements are, at their core, also all about results: wondering what will happen if the outcomes don't turn out to be what you want them to be.

A final warning about results-oriented goals: If they occupy too much of your headspace when entering a competition, you will be playing right into mind chatter's hands. In other words, if both you and your chatter are only thinking about outcomes, who is available to focus on those all-important, controllable aspects of the game that can contribute to a favorable outcome? Nobody, that's who. It is important to avoid being your chatter's co-conspirator.

ACTION GOALS

The opposite of results-oriented goals are *action goals*. These do not tend to receive as much attention because they are harder to observe or measure. They are not as exciting to think about as those big wins, personal records, and podium ceremonies. Still, they hold the keys to unlocking your performance potential.

Action goals are detailed strategies to which you can deliberately pivot your focus in order to enhance performance. If done right, such goals will have you thinking primarily about moment-to-moment specifics. For example, if you are a swimmer, you might want to focus on pushing harder off the wall and/or reaching farther with every stroke because these movements usually result in faster swimming times. If you are a fencer, you might attend to your strategies for parrying your opponent, such as moving your wrist a certain way to block your opponent's blade. If you are a basketball player, you might focus on opportunities to drive to the basket when you see the defense lagging. Notice these goals are under the athlete's control and are *not* about either short- *or* long-term results. They are geared toward immediate, potentially game-enhancing tactics.

Bulletproof competitors, such as NFL kicker Justin Tucker, have a mental game plan that includes regularly dialing into their action goals. Tucker, who plays for the Baltimore Ravens, said what helps him most in high-stakes moments is "focusing on the nuts and bolts of what's going to make the kick." He is a self-described "system kicker" who tells himself his "feelings don't matter" until "after the fact"—that is, after the kick does or doesn't go through the uprights (Highlight Heaven, 2022).

It's not that he's pretending his feelings don't exist. Rather, as I explained in chapter 5, he is "parking" them, effectively managing his chatter so he can turn his attention to his action goals. He knows just what specific, controllable actions to focus on when he sees the ball hiked and then spotted by the holder. From there, Tucker says, it is almost as if "the ball kicks itself" (Highlight Heaven, 2022).

Sport and performance coaches might say Tucker is demonstrating that he prioritizes his "process goals" or "learning goals." These are similar to action goals in that they don't emphasize thoughts and feelings, setting them apart from results-oriented goals. I use the term action goals to refer to this category of objectives because I want athletes to think specifically about what *action*—as opposed to what feeling or thought—is needed in the moment to improve performance. The fundamental difference between action goals and results-oriented goals is that action goals orient you to controllable, in-the-moment technical and/or strategic areas to improve, whereas results-oriented goals have you concentrating on *possible* outcomes.

Intentionally focusing on immediate, sport-specific actions pushes chatter into the background. Remember, you can't be thinking about two things at once. As Kobe Bryant said, what can separate you from the rest is your ability to keep your focus on the task at hand, not the end result. He defined mental toughness as the ability to "take your mind some-place else and concentrate on that other thing to the point where the thing that was bothering you is no longer a focus" (Sky High, 2022). Of course, he wanted to win the game and dominate his competition, but that would not happen if he zeroed in only on the box score. Kobe knew prioritizing the game's outcome would distract him from immediate action and turn up the volume on his chatter.

Of course, the actual content of your action goals will vary—as will what your chatter says to you. If you are a squash player, your chatter will distract you from thinking about volleying the ball, even if that is a major area you have been working on. If you are a faceoff specialist in lacrosse, and your key to high performance involves keeping your eye on your stick—not your opponent's—the first thing chatter will do is try to pull your attention away from this specific action and draw it to what your opponent is doing. Concentrating on a rock-solid set of action goals does not eliminate mind chatter, but it is your best bet for staying focused on the aspects of performance that you control.

The Nuts and Bolts

Now let's look closer at how to set action goals. To help you crystallize your in-game thought process, let's start where I often start with clients—namely, making sure you have a good handle on what you are currently working on in practice. I am suggesting you see your next event as an opportunity to improve in those small areas you or your coach have been prioritizing during training. Yes, you want to get on the podium or score in double digits. When game day rolls around, however, I want you to be "competing to improve"—thinking small even when the moment feels big.

Perhaps instead of "competing to improve," as I suggest, you have been "competing to prove"—viewing competitions primarily as a chance to impress others by putting up big numbers or placing near the top. If so, you may have found that this generates increased pressure, putting the focus squarely on results-oriented goals and others' judgments of you. In other words, you are creating the perfect environment for mind chatter to thrive. Adopting an "improvement mindset" instead will help release the pressure valve because it accounts for mistakes, even in tournaments, considering them occasions for progress. This turns questions of what others might think into a chattery sideshow that is not worth your time or attention.

In terms of where you might want to improve, your goals depend on the sport and your strengths. If you are a field hockey goalie, you might want to focus on coming out of the net sooner or improving your footwork. A cross-country runner might work on holding back for the first mile or keeping their shoulders lowered when they run. I am looking to help you build a connection between the improvements that you work on in training—physical actions and/or in-game strategies—and the very action goals you set for competition.

Clients tell me they could generate a long list of what they need to improve. The trick is to boil it down to the top two or three items that seem to be the most essential to improving current game-day performances. Let's be clear: These small, subtle shifts in focus can lead to the largest performance improvements.

Here are some more examples of useful action goals:

1. As a tennis player, you might set your action goal around coming to the net when the right opportunity presents itself.

2. As a golfer, you might be focused on keeping your head down when you putt.

3. As a figure skater, you might work on driving with your legs before you jump.

4. As a swimmer, you might work on pushing off the wall with full force every time you make a turn.

During play, I encourage you to gently remind yourself to focus on these small areas. If you need to drive with your legs or keep your head down, you can cue yourself to get your mind and body aligned with these areas of improvement.

PUTTING INTO PRACTICE

Diane was a college sophomore living her dream of playing for a prestigious Division I basketball program. She was struggling to figure out why, unlike in her previous season, she was so nervous during games and so upset with herself when she made a mistake. She told me, with a tear in her eye, "I'm just not the same player I was last year." In her freshman season,

Diane had been the only individual in her graduating class to get playing time. She realized that by virtue of being "just a freshman," she'd had the freedom to play without the weight of heavy expectations. She'd also had a stellar high school career, rarely struggling with any mental blocks because most of the time she was bigger, stronger, and more skilled than her opponents. She said mistakes back then were no big deal, but now they seemed catastrophic. Diane's college coach confirmed this change, telling me "I've never seen Diane so deflated."

The problem, as Diane described it, was that she didn't "want to let anyone down." We spent several sessions talking about how her fear of disappointing others and needing to prove that she deserved her scholarship were classic mind chatter-based fears. Diane also worried about what others might say about her after a poor performance. She then corrected herself, saying "my *mind chatter* worries about what everyone is going to say." That stroke of self-awareness, in which she distinguished her mind chatter from her own voice, deserved a major high five!

After several sessions, Diane was better able to "name" her chatter—a productive step toward "taming" it. What's more, she seemed to be grasping the concepts of "letting chatter be" and "making room" for it. So we entered the next phase of our work, focusing her mind on small, controllable aspects of the game. Her goal-setting strategy had previously been to focus on broad, undefined targets, such as "giving 100 percent" and "not messing up." However, she now understood that those goals were too general to be useful.

I asked Diane to pick two aspects of her game that she wanted to improve when she experienced the heavy weight

2. *Reminders, Reminders, Reminders*

Now that your list of front-pocket goals is ready to go, you need to figure out how you are going to remember them while you are out on the court, at the field, in the arena, or by the pool. I encourage you to write them down, more than once, before the event, and consider sticking them in your actual front pocket to help you remember. Or, write a note on a part of your body, like your arm or wrist. You could write your key action words on a racquet, water bottle, or sneakers—anywhere to help you remember.

By writing down your action goals, you are also taking responsibility for how your mental game will unfold. You are proactively taking a step toward what you deem important to you and your game, simultaneously pushing chatter and other worries down on the importance list. You own these goals; they are yours, and you will do everything you can to see them through. When the game is over, win or lose, you will take pride in that you did what you could to make yourself a better performer.

3. *Make Peace with Your Chatter before Setting Goals*

Be sure to have already "shaken hands" with your chatter and worked out a solid peace agreement before you say your action goals aren't working. A common mistake athletes make is assuming goal setting is useless without ever factoring mind chatter into the equation. In other words, they give up on the concept of goal setting without actually giving it a fair shot. The bottom line is the value of your action goals is proportional to how effectively you manage your chatter. If your goal setting strategies aren't working, I recommend going back to chapters 4 and 5, reading through the text, and working through the exercises I recommended for mind chatter management. There's nothing wrong with retracing your steps to gain a deeper understanding of this new approach.

4. Improving Versus Proving

Earlier in the chapter, I discussed the concept of "competing to improve." I want to emphasize an additional benefit of this strategy. When you consider the amount of pressure generated by the alternative approach, "competing to prove," it's clear that adopting a mindset that *doesn't* have you putting your entire worth on the line will free up some mental energy, giving you a bigger chance for a better and more pleasurable experience.

At your next game, I want you to focus on making small improvements in key performance areas; this will afford you the ability to appreciate smaller gains, affirming that you are on the right path toward increasing mastery of your craft. The following chart sums up the distinctions between the *improve* and *prove* approaches:

about the courage they would need for the triathlon to thinking about the courage needed to battle a serious illness. We reminded them of the courage they had already shown by attending this triathlon camp! They chose to put themselves in a position that was filled with more uncertainty and heart-pumping situations than most had ever experienced. After the workshop, one participant said she felt relieved that she did not have to feel confident because she "sure as hell was petrified." She took our advice and began treating the boot camp weekend as one big, albeit scary, adventure. By the end of the second day, she was riding around those cones and looking like she'd been doing it for years—regardless of how she felt inside.

THE COURAGEOUS MINDSET

Why did the triathletes sign up to take such terrifying risks? They wanted to explore their capabilities, an endeavor that does not lend itself to confidence but certainly requires courage. Courage is a willingness to take on the unknown, one step at a time, without knowing whether one's efforts will lead to success or failure. Courage helps you take the new chipping technique you've been working on in practice and try it out during a real golf round. Courage helps you keep up a fast pace when running a 5K when you have only maintained that speed during group training runs. The bridge from the work you've done in practice to the goals you set in your competition is paved with courageous action. That's why I trademarked the mantra that now serves as the title of this book: "Courage over Confidence."

If you are wondering if this approach is for you, know that *everyone* has the option to choose courage. You already do when you show up for Saturday morning practice after playing horrendously the day before. You choose courage when you continue to play hard even though your team is getting crushed. I said earlier that courage is a commitment; it is also, always, a choice. Consider big wave surfers who choose to confront uncertainty every day. They pick the biggest, gnarliest waves, and ride them without any true assurance that they will actually *live* to celebrate their accomplishments. These surfers put everything on the line and serve as an example—however extreme—of athletes who move confidence aside as they bravely choose to face their fears. In other words, they are not banking on confidence. They are fully focused and committed.

PUTTING IT INTO PRACTICE

At the triathlon boot camp previously mentioned, we led the triathletes in an exercise where we provided the prompt "In the face of chatter, I will courageously focus on..." and asked participants to finish the statement. Their answers helped us see whether they really understood how to apply the small, actionable goals they were setting or whether they were at risk of slipping back into a focus on results-oriented goals. For example, the biking goal of "looking forward instead of down" was the sort of controllable action that would be of use; on the other hand, a goal such as "don't fall" was liable to generate the sort of stiffness that would make losing balance *more* likely. We were hammering home the message that when the moment feels big, it is time to think small.

Take a few minutes to write down your answers to the same prompt: "In the face of chatter, I will courageously focus on..." Consider that list, along with your front-pocket goals from chapter 6, as two of your go-to inner-game tools.

In the face of chatter, I will courageously focus on...	
In the face of chatter, I will courageously focus on...	
In the face of chatter, I will courageously focus on...	
In the face of chatter, I will courageously focus on...	

A tennis player I worked with wrote the following after the prompt "In the face of chatter, I will courageously focus on...":

- Swinging **up,** and using my top spin on my ground-strokes (against my tendency to just push the ball back over the net).

- Throwing a **high** ball toss to get power on my serve (against my tendency to rush the serve and make a bad toss).

- Bouncing on my **toes** no matter the score (against my tendency to be flat footed if the match isn't unfolding according to plan).

The words in bold represented the key action word she used in matches. Focusing in this way—on a specific word within a specific goal—may help you, as it helped her, to keep your head in the moment. When playing against tough opponents and in high-pressure situations, the tennis player found that making the courageous effort to focus on these small goals kept her from mentally "checking out" the way she used to when the stakes felt too big to handle.

IS CONFIDENCE EVER HELPFUL?

You might be wondering if I think the whole concept of confidence in sports should just be thrown out. Isn't it okay to feel confident sometimes? Surely, confidence fits somewhere in the competition picture.

Confidence does have a place in your performances. Athletes tend to encounter two kinds of confidence: *post-success* confidence and *low-stakes* confidence. Post-success confidence is the feeling of self-assurance that *follows* a "winning" performance. For example, *after* a successful tryout, or when you return uninjured from your first post-surgery practice. You may walk a little taller and feel more self-assured after those successes. Before these experiences, however, your confidence may have been quite a bit lower because the risk of getting cut from the team or having an injury recur is seriously scary.

Low-stakes confidence, on the other hand, is when the chatter dial is turned down and you play without the fear that "everything is on the line." For example, if you are a squash player ranked top five in your age group, and you play against someone who picked up a racquet less than a year ago, it goes

CHAPTER 8

PUTTING IT TOGETHER

You can choose to take courageous action even when mind chatter tries to convince you there's no hope. Of course, it would be easier if you could just walk out onto the field and play without needing to make a mental game plan, manage your chatter, or find your sense of bravery. The good news, however, is now that you know what is holding you back—a hyperactive, chattery mind—you can efficiently shift your focus to solutions and away from problems. You are clearer about what is needed to become a mentally tougher competitor, courageously venturing into the land of uncertainty and high stakes as you go step-by-step through your plan of (1) expecting chatter, (2) making room for it, (3) setting specific action goals, and (4) practicing courage.

But applying what you have learned in your next big tournament and having everything "click" on the first try isn't actually how this process works. Just like you wouldn't automatically start making three-pointers in basketball if you had never practiced shooting from that distance, successful mind chatter management often takes time and intentional training. Some of you will find your rhythm quickly, becoming experts in "letting chatter be, so it will let you be" before long.

For most, however, getting the hang of this approach is like learning a new language. It requires patience and practice to understand and apply correctly.

Consider the following case examples. Amy was a high-level soccer player hoping to eventually make an Olympic team, and Ross was a high school swimmer hoping for college recruitment. I worked with them in distinct ways to teach them strategies to manage their mind chatter.

Amy was able to apply the mind chatter concepts very quickly. She easily made connections to what she was learning and put them to use almost immediately. On the other hand, Ross needed some additional tune-up sessions to help him appreciate the depths his chatter would go to warn him of potential disaster. Ross's case is the more common one; like most athletes, he needed to be reminded of a few mind chatter fundamentals, including how he could be nervous and still give it his all. Here are the details.

Case #1: Amy

Amy was an Olympic-caliber soccer player who had not experienced much mind chatter earlier in her career. She described playing with confidence during high school and throughout her first two years of college. Now, however, in her junior year, she was seeking help because she had become consumed by doubt and her play had become decidedly erratic.

Amy had been invited, for the second year in a row, to train with the Olympic development team along with other women who were vying for the opportunity to compete in the Olympics.

When she and I met, she was experiencing "tons of worry and fear" at the prospect of returning to the same field with the same coaches as the previous year, where she had fallen short of getting a shot to make an Olympic team. Typically, Amy approached any soccer competition with confidence and excitement. Now, she reported having trouble eating and sleeping, and uncharacteristically, she was spending long periods of time in her dorm room and less time hanging out with her friends.

Amy confessed that she had considered refusing to compete or faking an injury to get out of the tryout. She thought if she had a sprained ankle, nobody could blame her for not making the team. This was when her parents and her college coach encouraged her to reach out for help.

Regarding her prior Olympic camp tryout experience, Amy said, "You are going to laugh, but I was performing well right up until the coach told me I was doing well. At that moment, I totally lost my grip and played crappy for the rest of the time." Amy said that instead of "just playing," all she could think about was that she might never make it to the Olympics. In her mind, she was the worst player out there, although she recognized that several other players were not getting much playing time either.

Amy told me she really did want to try out again, but she wasn't sure anything could be done to help her "get rid of these awful feelings." I told her I had a plan in mind. We started with debunking the idea, which comes up frequently in my work with athletes, that she had a mental or psychological "disorder." Amy was convinced that because she "got so nervous" just thinking about trying out again, there must be something clinically wrong with her. She laughed when

I told her the only thing I could "diagnose" was a textbook case of mind chatter, and the good news was that she could be taught to manage it. I suggested her chatter had foiled last year's tryout; if she let it, it would disrupt the next one, too.

I explained to Amy how chatter works, including how it always shows up when we least want to hear from it. Amy agreed with my assessment that she was a very hard worker on the field and in the gym, but she had not put much time into advancing her mental game. Thus, it was understandable that she would feel unprepared and overmatched by doubts and second-guessing because those thoughts seemed to come out of nowhere.

A key step in helping any athlete with their chatter is getting them to see how predictable those naysaying thoughts really are. To prove this, I demonstrated that I could correctly guess most of Amy's chattery thoughts before she even identified what they were. I wrote my guesses, in big and bold letters, on my whiteboard. Amy was impressed at my accuracy. I wanted her to see that because the script was mostly set, she could start planning for mind chatter now, even though the tryout was still a month away.

Here is some of what I wrote:

- "What if I don't make the cut?"

- "What if Kennedy makes it and I don't?"

- "What if these coaches wish they had never invited me back?"

- "What if I start making mistakes?"

Amy could see in black and white how inevitable and universal chatter is, and why I considered it the likely culprit of her frustrations. She said the only thing I had left off the list was her fear of completely embarrassing herself.

I knew we were making meaningful progress when, after staring at the whiteboard for a bit, Amy paused, turned to me, and said, "So my chatter is not really about soccer. Is it?" She was putting it together, understanding that chatter's job was not to help her be a better competitor but to protect her from failures it perceived to be just as life threatening as an attack by a wild animal, as if there was no way a person could "survive" something like a second bad tryout.

In reality, Amy didn't have to worry about a lion mauling her in the jungle, but she agreed it did feel at times like she was in some sort of life-or-death jeopardy. I acknowledged how normal those fears were, and I asked her to do something that was bound to sound strange to a hard-nosed athlete like her. I told her we weren't going to wish her chattery thoughts away or think positive thoughts to drown them out, but we were going to grant those fears and doubts permission to just "be there."

As I often do, I spread my arms out wide to illustrate the concept of "making room" for chatter. So much of what mind chatter centers on is not the playing of the game but rather the consequences of not playing well. Amy agreed that she needed to be less focused on the doom-and-gloom predictions of her chatter and more focused on specific actions, such as getting a good first touch on the ball and making accurate crossing passes. We spent some time reviewing potential action goals and wrote them down on the whiteboard so they could be given priority.

Amy liked the concept of "making room," and the idea of comparing chatter to a waterfall resonated with her in particular. Instead of standing under the waterfall and getting "drenched in doubts," she would imagine taking a step back and letting the water fall in front of her. This exact image was what Amy thought about when she needed to remember how much energy she was wasting trying to control that which she could not. She loved the idea of gently stepping back to avoid getting soaked.

At the previous tryout, Amy had told herself to "just stay positive," which in her heart, she knew was an attempt to trick herself into thinking "better" thoughts than she was actually having. For instance, she reminded herself that the Olympic development coaches wouldn't have invited her to join the team if they didn't think she was good enough to be there. "Honestly," Amy said, "that worked for me in college and every other team I've played on." This is a common theme in my work. Athletes need help seeing that changing their competitive mindset needs to take into account the changes that have already occurred in their expectations, the stakes, and themselves.

I could tell Amy was racking up a few "aha" moments during our meetings. I wanted her to recognize that while she should be focused on action goals in her next tryout, her chatter would be fighting to be the focus of her attention. I knew it was helpful for athletes to learn through visual mediums, so I divided my whiteboard into two columns: "Soccer (Action)

Goals" and "Amy's Mind Chatter." You can follow along with this exercise, using your own action goals and mind chatter, by scanning the QR code below.

Soccer (Action) Goals	Amy's Mind Chatter
• Keep my head up • Have a good first touch • Communicate with teammates • Full-out hustle	• What if I don't make the cut? • What if Kennedy makes it and I don't? • What if these coaches wish they never invited me back? • I cannot make mistakes, but that's so hard to do. • What will people think if I don't have a good tryout? • What if I'm not as good at soccer as everyone else thinks I am? • What if I totally embarrass myself?

The action goals were items such as remembering to keep her head up, having a good first touch, communicating with her teammates, and remembering to always hustle. We broke these goals down even further, so she had just one or two words she could keep uppermost in her mind. Under the heading "Amy's Mind Chatter" was the mind chatter list I had created earlier, plus the following items Amy added herself: "What will people think if I don't have a good tryout?" and "What if I'm not as good at soccer as everyone else thinks I am?"

In a flash, Amy could see the distinction between these two completely different sets of goals. One set would help her be the best player she could be. The other would distract her with the possibility that her soccer career was about to go up in flames. Amy knew her attention should be on her small action goals rather than her mind chatter. I pointed to the chart and emphasized, "Remember, you are not your chatter."

I added one more idea to this conversation. Next to our chart, I wrote the heading, "*Why* is Amy trying out?" I asked Amy to share her reasons why—despite all the nerves, frustration, and fears—she was taking advantage of this tryout opportunity. She paused and then responded with tears in her eyes, "Ever since I was a little girl playing soccer, I dreamt of representing the United States. I'm so close now. I don't want to give up." She said she considered it a privilege to compete alongside such amazing women, whom she admired both for their talent on the pitch and their qualities as friends. She was motivated by the fact that they would help make her a better player *and* person. She cited other reasons too, such as her love of travel and the joy she felt when playing in front of big crowds. We listed those responses on the board and compared them to what mind chatter's message was for her. She was interested in discovering how good she could be, and the best place for that to happen would be surrounded by other talented athletes.

notebook that he had been wasting energy in the pool trying to control the uncontrollable.

Despite his swimming experience, Ross wasn't sure what to prioritize when it came time to discuss his action goals. He came up with two words, "head" and "core," that could serve as reminders of his "front-pocket" goals. These words corresponded to areas his coach had repeatedly told him he needed to work on. The word "head" referred to aligning his head properly in the water and keeping it steady, and "core" referred to using his abdominal muscles when kicking, building power from the center of his body.

The following week, Ross had his first race of the season. He said it was "okay." He admitted he felt pretty nervous, and although he told his chatter to "leave him alone," it "wouldn't go away." He thought the two action goals he had picked were useful. Overall, he gave himself a "B-" grade, compared to the "D" he felt he deserved for his previous race. Ross thought just having a plan and some focusing goals had made a difference.

I was pleased to see Ross trying to embrace some of the concepts we worked on, but he was still treating chatter as an unwelcome guest—someone or something for him to get rid of. The transition from resisting chatter to permitting it to be there is not an easy one for athletes to make; the typical response is to avoid the negative or combat it with positive self-talk. I was asking Ross to do the opposite. I told him to notice the negative thoughts, welcome them, and give them a seat on the couch while he prepared to swim.

We did an exercise to help Ross fully appreciate the extent to which chatter would go to instill fear in him, both before and during race day. Like many, Ross was not fully aware of how much damage chatter was "willing to do." The more aware he could become of what his scripted chattery lines would say, the less surprised he would be when he heard them on race day. I wanted Ross to strengthen his self-awareness muscles.

So I presented Ross with a list of fifty or so possible mind-chattery concerns competitive swimmers of his age and ability might have. It can be helpful for athletes to see such concerns laid out in this way, including some thoughts they may not have realized they were having. Ross's job was to mark all the concerns that applied to him. To view the list yourself and note which concerns apply to you, scan the QR code below. Be sure to open the link in the Google Docs app to access a dynamic checklist.

Ross was shocked to see he had checked off so many mind-chattery worries. He realized he wasn't just nervous about going fast or faster than his teammates. From the list I provided, here are several he identified as relevant to him. Ross's chatter wanted him to:

- be better than I was last week

- prove I am faster than I was last year

- try and impress the college coaches

- meet expectations

- make sure I place in my next race

- drop my time

- protect my reputation

- please my coach

- not disappoint my parents

- worry if I am wasting my life swimming all the time

No wonder Ross was struggling. It was as if he had been swimming with one hundred pounds of psychological weight on his shoulders. These were legitimate concerns, and anyone would feel intimidated if future-oriented worries like these were going through their minds while they tried to race. But I reminded him they were triggered by the uncertainty and high stakes, and if he could recognize that our work centered on changing his relationship to those doubts, he could instead focus on his action words—"head" and "core."

Ross and I had reviewed the notion of "courage over confidence," and he could now see how this fit into his mental game plan. He better understood the need to act with courage when the tsunami of mind chatter appeared. Ross was used to operating from the "If I don't feel right, I won't swim right" way of thinking. Now, he was learning he could feel less than perfect and still execute his swim plan.

I urged Ross to rehearse his mental plan even during practice sessions. One idea was for him to take the lead during swim sets, rather than letting others do so, even if the stroke the coach called for wasn't his best, and even if his teammates would eventually pass him. I wanted Ross to be "all in" on his willingness to allow chatter to visit. For someone who worried about what others thought of him as much as Ross did, this was a big ask; Ross viewed the idea of being passed by teammates as "scary." But this was the work needed to win the mental game, and it was time to start treating practice as a dress rehearsal for actual races.

The goal was to remain focused while he swam, knowing chatter would find various ways to distract and discourage him. We went through the script of what chatter would tell him. When—not if—those voices came, Ross had to learn not to be surprised. Rather, he should respond to the arrival of his guests with a casual response along the lines of "Oh, I knew you would come knocking. I've made room for you over there." Would he feel entirely comfortable doing this? Probably not. Could he make a commitment to do it anyway? Yes, he could.

I also made an audio recording for him to listen to pre-race. I reminded Ross that all of those uncomfortable thoughts and feelings he was having were completely normal, and he should find a spot on the pool deck for them to "hang out." I went through some other tips as well, reiterating the limitations of confidence and reminding him that his job in this next race was to try and improve on how well he could execute his action goals.

After his next race, Ross sent me a note saying he swam his best time. He was happy and appreciative. I wrote back, applauding his persistence, "You might not think of yourself as a great performer yet, but you sure are a courageous one!"

FINAL THOUGHTS

In these final pages, I will list the four steps I have presented in this book and the main takeaways for each. You'll know you have absorbed these messages when you no longer feel the need to run or hide from your self-doubts, second-guessing, or negative thinking. Nor will you consider mind chatter a sign that you and everything you worked so hard to achieve are in jeopardy. In time, your courage to perform will eclipse any concerns you have about not feeling confident enough to be successful. With these methods, you are ready to become the great competitor you always hoped you could be.

Here are the four steps and the major takeaways:

1. Expect and plan for mind chatter's arrival on the scene.

   - You have as much control over chatter showing up as you do over how tall you are. Anytime you face the combination of uncertainty and high stakes in competitions, you need to anticipate the arrival of a judgment- and failure-fearing voice warning you of trouble.

   - However, if you can anticipate that dialogue, you can stay one step ahead of it. Chatter rarely generates original material. Its lines tend to repeat themselves, always having to do with the same key concerns.

When you can anticipate the horrible, dramatic lines chatter will utter, you will avoid spending excess energy fighting a battle you cannot win.

2. "Make room" for your chatter instead of resisting its message.

- Developing a welcoming relationship with your chatter sounds radical until you consider the alternative, which is battling your chatter only to lose, again and again. This new way of looking at chatter has you treating it more as a friend, albeit one that can be annoying. The old method of fighting and resisting it has only made you more jittery. It is time to end the war.

- Thanking chatter for sharing, giving it a job to do, or noticing it without overreaction really helps. Why? Because you are accepting, rather than changing, the way you feel at that moment and in that particular competition. The rule is: Make room for chatter and get on with the show.

3. Identify and focus on specific, controllable "action goals."

- Results-oriented goals are important, but only up to a point. If given too much importance, they can get in the way. The risk of thinking only about these types of goals is that you and chatter, in lockstep, will be zeroing in on what might happen in the future instead of what needs to be done right now. You want to make peace with mind chatter but not an alliance.

- Action goals, on the other hand, are specific steps you can take to enhance your game. An effective action goal is one you can demonstrate to someone else. Ineffective action goals are those that are too vague or general, such as "trying to play well" or "giving it my all." Note that you would have a hard time showing someone what those nonspecific goals mean. When it is game time, keep your action goals in your front pocket and keep any results-oriented goals tucked into your back pocket.

4. Seek to perform with courage even when confidence is lacking.

- A big part of winning the mental game involves treating courage as more important than confidence. Fear, by definition, always precedes courageous action, so consider your second-guessing and performance anxiety as opportunities to be courageous.

- The challenges you seek aren't worthwhile if you already feel confident about achieving them. You choose them *because* of the risks they present. If I waited to feel confident skiing down a steep tree run that I'd never skied before, I would still be on the mountaintop. Instead, I courageously point my skis down the mountain; after I finish the run, I have some more confidence to try it again.

By learning to manage your mind chatter, you give yourself a greater chance of becoming faster, stronger, more resilient, and more mentally tough than ever before. You have a proven strategy to follow that will help you get to that next level of performance. One Olympic runner I worked with recognized he did not need to be running to improve his speed. He appreciated the in-office lessons on the mental game and recognized their benefits. He told me, "Every time we talk, I get faster!"

Perhaps the biggest benefit is that you will finally have a mental game plan that does not require you to hide or feel embarrassed about your performance. You can give up the notion that having such feelings makes you a coward or a wimp. I want every athlete to learn to embrace the courageous part of themselves and go out on the field ready to see their hard work pay off. Countless numbers of clients—from high school quarterbacks to professional basketball players and Olympic swimmers—have found these four steps to be an essential part of their success, transforming their game and their lives. I want the same for you.

ACKNOWLEDGMENTS

I owe a debt of gratitude to everyone who supported me throughout my book writing journey.

First, this book would not have been possible without the masterful guidance and editing of Jay Efran, PhD—my mentor and friend. Jay has been steadfast in my life since graduate school, where he was my professor. This book reflects what Jay taught me; that is, to always challenge accepted norms and view client problems through a fresh set of eyes.

Years ago, when I told Jay I was thinking about shifting the focus of my practice from clinical work with kids and families to sport psychology, he didn't blink. He encouraged me to enter the burgeoning field. Any courage I have shown in charting my career path has been with Jay behind me, pushing me to take risks and break barriers. And so it was, with Jay's unwavering support, I undertook this endeavor.

He helped shepherd this book through each stage, from rough draft to final draft. He challenged me to clarify concepts and ensure I said what I meant and meant what I said. He put up with me, reminding me countless times to drop the apostrophes and stop confusing "like" for "such as," and he never stopped offering assistance. On this book, and always, Jay has been for me what in sports we would call the ultimate clutch performer.

Another person this book project couldn't have done without is Greg Rubin, who provided exceptional editorial support. Every time I thought a sentence was crystal clear, Greg's keen eye spotted a way to improve it. Greg's skillful line editing and eye for organization and structure were invaluable, particularly during the final stages of the writing process. Greg was also full of fresh ideas and new ways in which I could help the reader understand the concepts I was teaching. We also had fun making sure we practiced what I was preaching, referencing to action goals and the word "elbow" every time we got distracted thinking about the end result instead of what needed to be worked on in that very moment. I am deeply grateful for his many contributions.

I also want to acknowledge with gratitude the Greenepsych team, particularly Lauren Ruhl and Milly Routledge, who were understanding of the time I needed to take away from my daily work at the office and who were sounding boards for many parts of the book. Their kindness and supportiveness are greatly appreciated.

Liia Richmond, who has been at the helm of Greenepsych's social media messaging and public relations efforts, is owed my sincere gratitude. Liia is a true professional, and if you heard about *Courage over Confidence* over the past year, either through a newsletter or online post, Liia was behind it.

Special thanks to those who read earlier drafts of several chapters, including Drs. Seth Gillihan, Erin Haugen, and Michael Sachs, as well as Amy Conway-Hatcher, Steve Kushner, Dan Cohn and Steve "Ollie" MacGregor. These colleagues and friends provided clear and concise feedback that found its way into the book.

This book is full of insights from my clients, who have trusted me with their personal concerns and sport psych challenges. I am in awe of the courage they have shown to manage their mind chatter to better themselves and those around them.

Additionally, I am deeply appreciative for the guidance and support provided by Ken Cain and Sherman Morrison at New Degree Press (NDP) and the entire NDP publishing team. They were an invaluable resource and helped make this book a reality.

I am most indebted to my family, who helped me realize this dream. Most importantly, thank you to my wonderful wife, Manon, who is the best teammate in life anyone could ask for. She was untiring in her support of me and this project. While I was writing about how people can manage their mind chatter, she was helping me with mine! Many early mornings and weekend writing sessions meant I wasn't doing much else other than book writing, but like she always does, she found a way to keep things light and fun. And, to my daughters, Tasha, Siobhan, and Gwen, who inspire me with their own accomplishments and keep me young at heart, thank you for your love, patience, and good humor throughout this long process. And to my mother, Rochelle Greene, and my sister, Ellen Berger, I am so lucky to have you both just one phone call away for extra doses of love and comfort.

Finally, thanks to my early supporters of *Courage over Confidence*. Their trust and encouragement helped make this book possible.

Lou Montresor	Ellen Berger
Dylan MacGregor	Jannell Kalifey
Denise Rodak	Justin Keen
Josh MacArthur	Hillary Wenner
Carol Bradbeer	Jessica Pfennig
Todd Burns	Becky O'Hara
Brody Ladda	David Lynch
Jeanna Vanni	Lauren Ruhl
Allison Miller	Nooha Ahmed-Lee
Lindsey Marshall	Malinda Ann Hill
Stacey Gross	Gavin Berger
Ann MacGregor	Mimi O'Grady
Susan Wagner	Rhonda Cohen
Tulug Ozdemir	Laura Pyott
Ellen Evans	Madison Cicone
Pamela Smith	Amy Conway-Hatcher
Steven Kushner	Fred Eisenberg
Jill Schardt	Stephen Zamulinsky
Maura Smith-Mitsky	Monica Bradbury
Amanda Nava	Neill Clark
Davis Woerner	Nathan Every

Josie Tomaino

Kristin Hoff

Erin Dougherty

Debbie Kelly

Rosemary Casey

Kimberly Bullock

Frances Gray

Madeline Maher

Kenyon Congdon

Jennifer Illig

Rochelle Greene

Sharron Russell

Mickie Simon

Erin Quinn

John Kepner

Nicole Wilkerson

David Byron

Andrew Baggaley

Shell Rummell

Cynthia Line

Joseph Garrett

Ross Berger

Patrick Santel

Lucy Brumberger

Joann Fegley

William Huffman

Quinn Magnus

Kate Livesay

Steve Rummel

Kristine Augenthaler

Dorothy MacGregor

Stacy Axelman

Heidi Meertz

Robin Ford

Mike Ford

Loryn Whitman

Josh Hillman

Jack Valentine

Joseph Ettorre

Lori Axelrod

Jennifer Maher

Gretchen Cooney

Juan Colina de Vivero

Melanie Joseph

Susan Shaw

Cyndi Rickards

Susan Damiano

John Gonzales

Joe Tuohey

Meghan Moore

Jeffrey Ford

Barbara Cleffi

Richard Adler

Gavin Sutherland

Nancy Kuhn

Paul Weldon

Michael Hanlon

Kevin Jackson

Boomer Dell

Marty Kupprion

ABOUT THE AUTHOR

Mitchell Greene, PhD, is a clinical and sport psychologist who received an undergraduate degree in psychology from Boston College and a PhD in clinical psychology from Temple University. He is the owner of Greenepsych Clinical and Sport Psychology, a psychology practice located in the suburbs of Philadelphia. Dr. Greene works primarily with athletes pursuing high performance goals as well as coaches and athletic departments seeking to educate student-athletes on mental health and performance enhancement strategies.

Dr. Greene's articles, blog posts, podcasts, and workshops have reached national and international audiences. His breadth of professional experience has made him a sought-after consultant to both individual athletes and high-performing coaches and teams.

Dr. Greene is married with three children. He stays active running and cycling. For more information about Dr. Greene and his practice, go to Greenepsych.com.

APPENDIX

INTRODUCTION

Greenberg, Jay. 1999. "Knoblauch Knows He's Replaceable." *New York Post*, October 22, 1999. https://nypost.com/1999/10/22/knoblauch-knows-hes-replaceable/.

Loughran, Colin. 2022. "Tua Tagovailoa Asked 'Do I Suck' during Dolphins Struggles." *New York Post*, November 28, 2022. https://nypost.com/2022/11/28/tua-tagovailoa-asked-do-i-suck-during-dolphins-struggles/

Minutaglio, Rose. 2022. "Mikaela Shiffrin Lost the Olympics but Won the World." *ELLE*, July 18, 2022. https://www.elle.com/culture/a40478203/mikaela-shiffrin-olympics-skier/.

CHAPTER 1

Bushnell, Henry. 2021. "Simone Biles, Katie Ledecky, and the Impossible Pressure of Greatness: 'A Blessing and a Curse.'" *Yahoo Sports*, July 28, 2021. https://sports.yahoo.com/simone-biles-katie-ledecky-and-the-impossible-pressure-of-greatness-a-blessing-and-a-curse-104735552.html.

Gould, Daniel. 2009. "The Professionalization of Youth Sports: It's Time to Act!" *Clinical Journal of Sport Medicine: Official Journal of the Canadian Academy of Sport Medicine* 19 (2): 81–82. https://doi.org/10.1097/JSM.0b013e31819edaff.

Güllich, Arne, Brooke N. Macnamara, and David Z. Hambrick. 2022. "What Makes a Champion? Early Multidisciplinary Practice, Not Early Specialization, Predicts World-Class Performance." *Perspectives on Psychological Science* 17 (1): 6–29. https://doi.org/10.1177/1745691620974772.

Hahn, Jason Duaine. 2020. "Olympian Mikaela Shiffrin on Dealing with Performance Anxiety: 'I Never Expected' It Would Affect Me." *People*, July 14, 2020. https://people.com/sports/mikaela-shiffrin-performance-anxiety-mental-health-heart-of-vail-valley/.

TEDx Talk. 2018. "How We Can Change Youth Sports Culture | Heather Bergeson | TEDxEdina." December 10, 2018. YouTube video, 14:24. https://www.youtube.com/watch?v=UrlPuRfoGdY.

CHAPTER 2

Covey, Stephen R. 1989. *The 7 Habits of Highly Effective People: Powerful Lessons in Personal Change.* New York: Free Press.

Ehrenreich, Barbara. 2010. *Bright-Sided: How Positive Thinking Is Undermining America.* First edition. New York: Picador.

Peale, Norman Vincent. 1952. *The Power of Positive Thinking.* New York: Prentice-Hall.

Wood, Joanne V., W.Q. Elaine Perunovic, and John W. Lee. 2009. "Positive Self-Statements: Power for Some, Peril for Others." *Psychological Science* 20 (7): 860–866.
https://doi.org/10.1111/j.1467-9280.2009.02370.x.

CHAPTER 6

Gallwey, W. Timothy. 1974. *The Inner Game of Tennis: The Classic Guide to the Mental Side of Peak Performance.* New York: Random House.

Highlight Heaven. 2022. "Justin Tucker Legendary Interview after UNREAL Performance." October 9, 2022. YouTube video, 1:38.
https://www.youtube.com/watch?v=ZBaA3lJQstM.

Sky High. 2022. "Mental Toughness—Kobe Bryant." April 23, 2022. YouTube video, 0:21.
https://www.youtube.com/watch?v=AA6qYmmDWXQ.

CHAPTER 7

Kamphoff, Cindra. 2022. "3 Mindsets That Separate the Best from the Rest with Dr. Alex Auerbach, Director of Wellness and Development, Toronto Raptors—Cindra Kamphoff." *High Performance Mindset.* Released August 18, 2022. Podcast, 49 min.
https://cindrakamphoff.com/
http-thehighperformancemindset-com-506-3-mindsets-that-separate-
the-best-from-the-rest-with-dr-alex-auerbach-director-of-wellness-and-
development-toronto-raptors/.

Made in the USA
Monee, IL
05 July 2024